ONLINE DATING GUIDE FOR LOVE SEEKERS

ANTHONY EKANEM

Made with ♥ on the Notion Press Platform
www.notionpress.com

Contents

Preface

Online dating is not all fun and games and there are a lot of things that a person has to know about online dating before one gets into the intricacies of it. Online dating may seem to be the simplest thing in the world but it is not. It should be viewed in all earnestness or things could go haywire. Every game has its rules; unless you know all the rules, you can't become a good player and eventually a winner.

There are so many kinds of people around. Just look around you - how many people you know look the same? The sizes, builds, shapes, and features are all different! And that is just about the external appearances. And when it comes to character, it becomes a very different story altogether. Take a trip down memory lane, go back to your classrooms, and look around.

A classroom is one place where we get to interact with a lot of different people on a very close basis. We get to rub shoulders and corners with very different people, and we get to know them on a one-to-one basis. So how many of your classmates did you genuinely like? I don't mean like them as classmates but as people. Was it easy to get along with all of them? That is why we often end up with best friends or clichés in classrooms.

We do not and do not have to like everybody. The tastes and interests of one person might match with ours while the tastes and interests of another person may be at complete loggerheads with ours. So, when it comes to dating, it is very much the same story. But over here, there are some strings attached. Unlike in a classroom contact, most people go on dates with a more impressive purpose, and that is to find a life mate. There are a hundred and one things that should match before two people decide to spend the rest of their lives with each other.

Many people think that they do not need any help with dating. They may be right because nobody knows a person's tastes and likes better than the person himself or herself. Maybe most of us do not need any help in making the right choice but isn't it good to get a few pointers on the dating process as such, particularly on online dating? It is with this objective that this book was written so that the thousands who are now availing of Internet dating may get the best out of it.

You can either use this book as a general guideline to streamline your match-hunting venture, or you can keep coming back to it to make sure of every step before you put your foot forward. I can promise you that if you use this book to guide you, there is *no need to fear at all...you won't stumble.*

THE FUNDAMENTALS OF ONLINE DATING

CHAPTER ONE

Understanding Online Dating

Online dating refers to websites that offer services to individuals or groups who wish to meet people online for social or romantic relationships. You dictate what type of relationship you are looking for which gives you complete control over whom you talk to and whom you don't.

Simply put, an online dating service is a community of people who gather to interact, socialize, and make friends with each other. Most hope that love will come their way through the site, but at the very least, they want to find a way to date a diverse and unique person they may not have the opportunity to meet in their "real lives".

There is a myriad of websites that cater to this service, and this is especially true for seniors. A quick search on the Internet will reveal an abundance of dating opportunities for those over 50. The process involved in meeting someone online can vary from site to site. The basic process for meeting another person online is for an individual to sign on to an online dating site by entering a unique username and password that applies only to that individual.

Some of these sites are free; others require you to pay a monthly membership fee. Almost all will give you a free trial period to see if you like the site and what it has to offer. You're probably going to have a better experience with a site that requires paid membership, but we'll address that a little later.

Once a person is signed up for the service, they are normally required to create a user profile, which involves filling out an electronic form that asks specific questions. These questions can range from geographical details to favourite food to sexual orientation.

You will also be asked what type of person you want to meet and what qualities you'd like for them to possess. You can also specify a geographical area you would like them to be from. A person's information is then entered into the site's database, and users have various ways of accessing another user's profile.

You may be able to create a personal profile as well that tells others specific details about you. This can include experiences or memories you might want to share as well as the dreams and goals you want to achieve. We have a separate section on the best way to create your profile so you can receive the best results. You will also be able to enter a photograph of yourself. Again, we touch on this later. A picture can be a great starting point to meeting that special someone though it's not the main point.

Users can also search an online dating site for a compatible match, which is determined by technological profiling of the information a user has supplied to the site. More commonly, users post photos of themselves on their profile to give others a general idea of their type. However, the online aspect of dating services normally requires users to judge one another on their ideas, how they present themselves, and the overall impression they give.

Physical presence rarely factors into making a connection with another person on the Internet, and this is no different for online dating. Once you have joined a senior dating website, you'll likely be invited to join chat groups, and you'll be able to search for other members meeting your criteria. You may even be able to fine-tune your criteria to find others meeting your initial criteria and that also share common interests or hobbies. You will be able to chat with a possible match and communicate with them through e-mail. When you decide to meet in person is all up to you!

Often, there is a sense of anonymity and mystery in meeting people online that is rare in meeting people. Online dating offers an alternative to the norm and is most likely appealing to those who are unlucky in real life when it comes to meeting romantic prospects. In addition, the common fear of rejection is less intense in an online environment, thereby, making online dating an attractive means of meeting others.

Online dating is a common and popular service for people to communicate with others, which includes finding love. This has been the most significant shift in American dating culture since the mid-1960s.

The Internet has offered additional functions that reduced the time for people searching for documents. Now, the Internet is not only for searching for information, but for also meeting friends, finding love, and finding people who share the same habits and religious beliefs. Online dating services facilitate these functions.

The most popular online dating website is match.com which is a public company that started in April 1995. In its 10-year history, more than 60,000 new people registered on Match.com every day, and it has grown to more than 15 million members with profiles posted, active users and about one million paying subscribers from more than 246 countries.

Now, there are numerous online dating websites on the Internet like match.com. They cater to all types of individuals and lifestyles and it's a great way to find someone with common interests. For seniors, the growing popularity of online dating services is stellar news! You can meet people from all over with just the click of your mouse. There are tons of sites specifically geared toward older people who want to find a date and that's even better news!

Many people think that online dating services are only for young people, but that couldn't be further from the truth. Times have changed and so have relationships. Back when the over-50 crowd was at prime dating age, a date consisted of two people meeting somewhere away from home. Dating couples typically went to the local diner or ice cream parlour where they shared a root beer float. The rules of society dictated that dating was to happen in public.

Today, however, dating has changed. There are still plenty of opportunities to date outside the home, but plenty of relationships have started right on the Internet surrounded by all the comforts of home. If nothing else, you can take comfort in knowing that there are hundreds and even thousands of single people over age 50 who are interested in dating or creating new friendships, just like you.

Is online dating really for you? We're willing to say yes, but let's look at the pros and cons just to be sure.

We, human beings, have been in this world for thousands of years. And since the beginning, people have been choosing their life partners. Cultures across the world are very different and we can come across so many ways in which people choose their life mates.

But the concept of finding a life partner with the help of the Internet is a recent concept when compared with the history of mankind as such. Of course, the Internet and computers have influenced man's life so much that it is no surprise that in the matters of finding a suitable partner too, the Internet has made its presence felt.

Online dating is, to put it very simply or flatly, finding a partner with the help of a machine namely the computer via the Internet. That, itself, makes the idea and the process a very novel one indeed, Hundreds of happy people across the globe have been successful in finding suitable partners by the means of online dating. But to be frank with you, a lot of not-so-lucky persons have been goofed and jilted by the same process. So, to make sure that you find a place in the first list, let us go into the details of online dating.

The Magic of the Internet

Everything that applies to the Internet, applies to Online dating as well. The Internet as we know allows for unlimited possibilities in communication, and it is this feature that has proved to be at the same time the biggest boon, as well as bane for online dating.

People can start from scratch and get to know everything about each other before the actual meeting takes place. Tastes and preferences, likes and dislikes, interests and obsessions can be discussed on a one-to-one basis so that when the meeting takes place these two people are not in the least strangers to each other. Wonderful, isn't it?

But at the same time, this possibility for unlimited communication leaves a lot of space for guile as well. Humanity is endowed with a remarkable ability to use, misuse, and abuse the same thing. And naturally, online dating too has been and is still being used for vile purposes.

The person who is misusing this facility may either be a practical joker or maybe someone with more devious intentions who is out to get some victims. It is because of this reason that a little bit of homework is good before you hit the road. But you do not have to worry, the homework has already been painstakingly done for you and all you have to do is run your eyes along the following lines and you will be all set to strike gold.

How Did Online Dating Become So Popular?

The reason is *simple*. It is very much the same reason that the Internet itself became so popular. The Internet opens a whole new world of communication and contact. And the reasons for this are given below.

Speed

Try to picture what used to happen earlier in the days when people had to depend on the good old postal system. During those days, a person had to wait for one or two days for a letter to get across to a person who lived in the same state itself. The second person in turn would take one or two days to respond and this letter would take one or two days to get back to the first person.

So, in effect, a single correspondence would stretch over a week. But now it's a different story. The time taken for the first letter and the response has been brought to two minutes! Waiting may make the heart grow fonder but e-mail makes two people get close faster!

Privacy

The Internet provides privacy too. One can carry out communication with another person in the absolute privacy of one's bedroom or bathroom or wherever one chooses to be. There is no fear of eavesdropping or overhearing. Thanks to e-mail and chat facilities.

Options and Opportunities

The Internet provides other options like voice chat or video conferencing and stops short only of the physical touch. But then who would want to start a relationship by touching right away? You can see a person, talk to a person, and listen to the person's voice, can you think of a better way to start a date?

Economy

Thanks to the Internet and the best part is that all this comes to you for a small sum. All you need is a PC and an Internet Connection and you are all set. The only thing more you could ask for is a step-by-step guide to finding your dream date ... well here it is! So, what are we waiting for?

Be Clear About What You Want

We all know that man is a social being. However, man is also a lonely being. (And when we say man, we mean women too). Man longs for company. The company not just from friends and family, but from that special person with whom he or she can share those sweet nothings, those simple pleasures and pains, someone with whom he or she can build a whole new life, someone with whom he or she can raise a family of his or her own.

Now, this is a fundamental need of man: to find a life mate. And the most popular method used for this is dating. When we talk about dating in the very finest sense of the word, please understand that dating is not to be viewed as a precursor for sleeping together. It is much more than that.

It is the first step towards choosing a life partner and online dating has made the whole process a lot simpler now.

Marriage Versus a Casual Relationship

Now, what you do and what you want is entirely your business. I don't want to sound nosey, but I would like to draw a fine line between the kind of dating that is involved in these two quests. Of course, we are all grown up and so let us act like grown-ups. In a casual relationship, we are looking for fun. And mind you, the fun can have a lot of connotations. So here the object of one's desire will be a person who is not inclined towards a serious relationship.

If both parties are of the same view, then it is well and good because they understand each other perfectly and do not expect much from such a relationship. This leaves no room for heartbreak. It is when one party is in for something more serious, and the other party is into sheer frivolousness that the problems start. So, you should be clear about what you are looking for from the start, and you should make your intentions very clear to the other person.

At the same time, you should have no doubts about the intentions of the other person as well. Remember, even if it is a casual relationship, there should be mutual understanding at least about the nature of the relationship. Of course, there is yet another possibility where a casual relationship can blossom into something more serious. But, again in such cases, it is your instincts that can help you identify what is good and what is bad.

No matter how strong a person is, anyone can be taken for granted. Being jilted is never a nice experience. So those of you who are going in for a casual relationship, for heaven's sake, be on your guard! Marriage is altogether a different story, but we will deal with that later.

Dating Comes from a Fundamental Need

Let's face it, sex is important, but sex is not the most important reason for dating. Maybe during the age of thoughtless youth, when new hormones are being pumped in and out, sex is on everyone's mind. But as one matures (mind you that does not mean growing old and grey) sex takes the back seat and mutual support, likes and dislikes, cooperation, caring, and sharing come to the forefront.

We start thinking about building up a world of our own and we need someone to share it with and not just someone to sleep with. Sex is a fundamental need of every human being. We all have it in us to give and receive physical pleasure. But when you sit and think about it for a minute, you can see that this urge is the result of another urge.

There is a primary urge in every human being to breed and produce offspring, and it is this urge that gives rise to such a powerful sexual desire. But whatever the urge, the most dignified means to satisfy it is dating. Nobody, not one of us, is complete without a partner; and it is to satisfy this need that people date. Because of this, the rest of this manual will be dedicated not to finding the right sex partner, but to finding the right life partner.

Online Dating Is Here to Stay

Let's accept the fact that dating couldn't get better. Online dating is the real thing. Let's compare it to the old system of evening balls or social gatherings. Imagine you are at this big gathering where there are a lot of men and women looking out for suitable partners.

Suppose you bump into one or two people with whom you seem to strike an immediate rapport. You are then able to take this person out onto a balcony with just the moon to keep an eye on you. You get to talk to this person for hours and hours; just talk and nothing else. You get to discuss likes and dislikes then finally when it is time to part you leave with a promise to meet the next day at an equally enjoyable spot. These talks go on for days and weeks and finally you decide that this indeed is the person with whom you want to spend the rest of your life. You start meeting in more open places, you hold hands and even kiss. You begin to go out for lunch and dinner and spend even more intimate time together. When the moment is right and your decision is made, it then becomes time for you to say, "*I do.*" *Sigh*! It sounds like a nice fairy tale, doesn't it?

Well, it needn't be. It could be your own love story because the concept of online dating is just what has been described above. If you click the right buttons everything could work out fine for you and we have evidence to prove it.

As I mentioned earlier, one of the best things about online dating is that it affords a lot of privacy. You can chat for hours, video conference, or do whatever it is you care to do without arousing the interest of others or attracting the wrong kind of attention. All you need is a computer and Internet access everything becomes as discreet as can be. But along with that, may I add that we need a little bit of common sense as well or else we might find ourselves within the clutches of many lurid monsters lurking out there.

Another good thing about online dating is that it saves a lot of money, otherwise, you would have had to splurge each time you took someone out on a date. It is for these reasons and many more personal reasons that thousands of people find online dating to be a great convenience.

Getting the Most Out of Online Dating

Many people who decide to give online dating a try often end up with their hair singed and their fingers burnt. The reason we decided to put together such a manual as this is that online dating is not as simple as it looks. You need to know how to go about it to get the best out of it. Most people do not like to take chances and when it comes to finding a life partner, people do not want to take chances at all.

But you can relax, for, through this manual, we will be dealing with all the do's and the don'ts and so the whole process will be quite easy and enjoyable for you. This manual will provide you with step-by-step instructions on how to go about online dating successfully.

We have no doubts about the decision-making abilities of our readers and so we do not propose to give a lot of advice on the issue. Our purpose is simply to provide a couple of guidelines which we hope our readers will find valuable as they proceed in the attempt to find the perfect partner.

CHAPTER TWO

Advantages of Online Dating

Dating, these days, is far different from how it was years back. People usually met at parties or were hooked up by friends. The couple would realize whether the friendship could go on to the next level or it was never meant to be. Meeting people online is like having friends doing all the work looking for that special someone. Recently, more people have had higher success rates in getting a date online than the conventional method.

To know more, here are some benefits which are interesting to know about online dating:

1. Safety

By personally signing up on an online dating service, you can meet many people without the risk of revealing your personal information. The only time that such details can be revealed will be done voluntarily by you or a potential partner when a level of trust has been established.

2. Security

Dating online is supposed to help people who have difficulty meeting that special someone. Some people take advantage of that and prey on innocent people so most dating sites have made a system that allows you to report a user and have that person blocked for malicious conduct and prevent this from happening to other people.

3. Affordable

Dating people is costly especially since you will probably go out on more than one date. By getting to know many people online, you will be able to save a lot of money since the same information that you gather online can be done just like going out on an actual date but without the cost of dinner, a movie, etc.

4. No more rejection and unwanted people

For men, dating online avoids the embarrassing experience of going up to meet a girl and getting rejected. By signing up for an online service and just chatting online, if you are turned down, you can easily forget about that person and meet someone new. For women, dating online helps avoid meeting the wrong person. It saves the time and effort of giving love to someone more deserving like that potential partner.

5. Openness

Most people find it difficult to talk to a stranger for the first time because there is the fear that the other person will not appreciate what is shown.

Since dating online provides a buffer by talking to someone via the computer and not face to face, another benefit is that you can be as open as you want to be without fear of showing any sign of emotional attachment.

Online dating can be fun. Whether it's just to meet new friends or meet that potential partner, you never know until you try. The possibilities are endless but don't concentrate too much on trying to force a love connection. It's better if you look at your online dating experience as the search for a date, not a mate. You'll be much more satisfied and less frustrated if your view is geared this way.

Since you'll be chatting with people online, let's look at ways you can figure out if the person you're communicating with is not telling the truth.

LIAR?

Online dating can prove to be a wonderful experience but you have to remember certain precautions in dating people over the Net. How would you know that the person you will be meeting for the first time is honest and is not deceiving you? Here are some tips to guide you.

First, listen to what your gut is saying. If something does not feel right when talking to the person, then most likely, something may indeed be wrong, and he or she is not saying the truth. If something triggers a red flag during communications, it is probably an indication to move on. Trust your instincts.

Again, we warn you not to give out your personal home information too early. If he or she is an honest person, he or she would understand this. He or she knows the danger that lurks in online dating, so it is just understandable that you take enough measures to protect yourself. He or she might admire you for that. It just shows that you are not that cheap and desperate in trying to hook up with dates.

If you think you have gathered enough information about your date, then you could try doing a background check on that person. If your date knew that you are giving him or her a background check, he or she won't make a big deal about it. After all, honest people don't have something to hide, do they?

There are plenty of online services that provide background checks of people, but they almost always charge a fee. You should be prepared for that and keep it in mind when you think this might be a step you'll want to take.

Keep in mind that there are people who lie about their profile and lie about the things they are saying over the Internet. Some lie about their marital status, some about their physical appearances, and some about their intentions. Be always alert. Not all people in online dating services are good people, but not all of them are bad either.

Trust your instincts. Hopefully, you find one over the Internet that is honest and has good intentions for you. He or she might be your destiny. Also, be careful of people who want to meet up with you instantly and pressure you to do so. If they bug you to give your contact details when they don't want to give you their personal contact information, stay away.

Another warning sign is that the person you are talking to is not consistent in giving you information about their marital status, age, employment, etc. You may notice conflicting information between conversations. This is a huge red flag. If somebody is bothering you by constantly sending you a multitude of e-mails or trying to contact you in person, stop sending him or her messages immediately. If the site will allow you to block them, do so to prevent any further harassment.

Unfortunately, it sounds like we're just focusing on the negative, but there are safety risks that you must be aware of when communicating with people through an online dating service. When you know what to look for, you can be more prepared to find that special someone and not that fake someone.

There are some ways that you can make yourself stand out to someone if you think you might be interested in dating them. Flirting in person is easy – flirting online is a little different.

CHAPTER THREE

Getting Started

It is always best to approach unfamiliar territory with caution. Be sure about yourself and be sure about what you want. Just because anyone and everyone can type out whatever they want in a chat room doesn't mean that we must do the same.

The Internet has the wonderful quality of being accessible to everyone. But this same quality attracts all kinds of people to it. But just because a lot of people who enter a chat room have only dirt on their minds, it doesn't mean that everyone is like that. If you stick to the class that you have and maintain your poise, you can indeed get the right kind of response.

There are a lot of nice people using the Internet, but it all depends on what you do. Do to others what you want them to do to you is the golden rule that applies here. There are no rules for the game. All are players out there. But just because others are ruffians, it doesn't mean that you must be one too. Your approach is the only thing that can get you the kind of response that you want.

I don't think it is very sensible to decide suddenly that you would like to use the Internet to get a date. By just entering a chat room and saying "I'm available" you are merely putting yourself up for sale and will most likely not get the results you desire.

One point that all of us must understand is that in a chat room, all are equal. Do not go by the misconception that entering a chat room is like sauntering into a ballroom dressed in your best. Then everyone turns to stare at you and the most eligible person (read that as the sexiest person of the opposite sex) catches your eye and makes his or her way towards you. That kind of thing happens only in James Bond movies, and we all know that James Bond never goes into a serious relationship. It's all fun and games for him.

Where Do You Start?

The first tip we would like to give you is not to go straight away into a singles' chat room and try to find somebody who would interest you. Many such chat rooms are virtually flooded with people who have only one thing on their minds - sex. So, no matter what you ask for, it always ends up in that and the purpose is defeated. You will never get the kind of person who will match your interests and tastes.

Sometimes it can get quite infuriating. Everything starts well. You are having a nice conversation with a person and warming up when suddenly, the topic moves towards the three-letter word. Then you let out a sigh and either must bar messages from that person and risk the person bad-mouthing you in a public chat room. Usually, you have to leave the chat room altogether.

In other words, it is the easiest thing to get someone to sleep with you but if you are looking for something more enduring, like a partner for life, then you are going to have to be a little more patient. The pick of litter is not easy to find. But you do find it; it is going to be worth the effort. So, instead of going into a singles' chat room, what you could do is try the whole thing out from a different angle. You could try working backwards.

More than Looks

Sit for a minute or two and try and think about the things that interest you and things that you would find interesting in a person. By 'things' over here I am not referring to physical attributes. I am not referring to something that might interest you in a person's physical appearance. Again, the distinction must be drawn between a serious relationship and a casual relationship.

In a casual relationship, the importance is always on physical attributes. We are more concerned with what the person looks like and what the person has been endowed with. On the other hand, if we have a serious relationship, then the physical qualities are not so important. Compatibility is probably the most important factor over here. Along with that, there are qualities that we will be looking out for. We are talking about the qualities of the mind. After all, beauty is only skin-deep!

This idea might sound strange, but it is true. The idea is that it is possible to grow to like the looks of a person. Once you find the character of the person agreeable you will start liking the person. It is entirely possible to fall in love with a person if the person does not look like a movie star. That is one of the tricks that nature plays.

Many people insist on looking at the other person's picture before committing to a relationship. They might have their reasons of course, but I, for one, feel that such a decision based largely on looks is more suitable for a casual relationship. It is bound to fizzle out after some time. After all, how long can you keep staring at a person? And what happens if the person doesn't stare back at you? Or even worse, what happens if you find the person staring at another person? Looks may be important, but they certainly are not the most important thing and should never be used as the deciding factor if you are thinking about a serious relationship.

Common Interests

A human being is not like a piece of glass through which you can look and see the other side. A human being is more like a diamond, which when held against light reflects and deflects light so that a myriad of colours is seen. We're complex.

We have a lot of interests and the interests of one person need not match the interests of another. But thankfully the interests are not as numerous as human beings. So, we are bound to find a lot of people who share our interests. And if we can find someone like that, then our search should end there. So, what are your interests? That is something for you to find out. Mind you, you might have to do some serious thinking before you level down your preferences. There might be a lot of things that you enjoy doing but about which you have given a second thought.

Your interests could be something like sports or outdoor activities. Or you could think of interests like social work or crosswords or religious interests. Keep the ball rolling; please understand that the words I have listed here are mere suggestions. Your tastes and interests could be very different. So let them be. And once you have decided on what your interests are, then half the story is done.

What Interests You In A Person?

This is probably the more important part of the story. Each one of us must sit and think about what we would like in another person. Having the same interests doesn't necessarily mean that you can get along with a person. For example, if you are a person who likes to talk a lot, it doesn't mean that you could like another person who likes to talk a lot as well. If two people try to keep talking at the same time then obviously, there cannot be any dialogue.

So also, if you are the silent, reserved type and the other person is also the silent, reserved type, there will hardly be any dialogue at all! The watchword here is "compatibility." The interests of partners should complement each other and not clash.

Keyword Searches

So now that you have decided what is it that interests you in a person and what your interests and tastes are, try such keyword searches on a search engine like Google.

The idea here is not to advertise yourself as a person who is in search of a life partner. No matter how well you put it, it loses that touch of subtlety once you are in a singles' chat room. So don't do it that way. You remember how we spoke about working backwards; this is how it is done.

We will tell you how to project yourself best in a later chapter but for now, let us talk about finding Mr Right or Miss. Right. An interesting thing to be noted here is that it is not difficult to fall in love with a person or to make a choice. The difficult part is to make the right choice and fall in love with the right person.

Likes versus Dislikes

The second thing that you could do is chalk out a list of qualities that you genuinely dislike in a person. Yes, I am not joking! Dislikes are just as important, or even more important than likes. We all must make compromises here and there, but if we start away by condoning things, which we genuinely dislike, it is going to tell on the relationship at some time or the other.

I would like to give a word of caution here. A lot of people make a mistake when they are courting. They put up their best behaviour, which is very good of course, but they try to be very adjusting and accommodating which is NOT very good. A point that they tend to overlook is that they are not going to be going on a camping trip with this person that they are trying to impress; they are going to be living the rest of their lives with the person.

So, it is best not to be "too *very accommodating and adjusting*." You can afford to stick to things that you are very particular about. And if you have any thoughts that you will be able to mould the person out of his or her offending habits later, forget it.

The moment you start trying to mould or cajole the person out of his or her habits, whatever they may be, the word becomes 'nagging' and if at all the person does drop the habit, he or she will love you less for it. It doesn't work that way. So, it's best to have a clear idea about qualities and habits that you genuinely dislike in a person and steer clear of the 'lesser mortals' who have those habits.

Once you have a clear idea about your likes and dislikes, you are in a better position to make the right choice. And considering the multitude of people out there, you do not have to worry or be over-anxious that you just might not find anyone at all. He or she is out there, and if you are doing what you are doing right, namely barking up the right tree you will succeed.

Some people even believe that everything is ordained. It has been written down who should marry whom and, in the end, only that which should happen will happen. Well, I don't know about that, but I do know that dating helps speed up the process. Another thing that you could do is you could just let nature take its course. Oh, nature has its wonderful ways. There is a lot of chemistry involved in the selection of a partner so maybe the best thing we could do is lend nature a helping hand.

Friends First

Try to look at this endeavour not as a prospective husband/wife hunt but as an effort to make a lot of friends, and I mean good friends. Friends that you can laugh aloud with, friends who make you laugh. Not everyone can make us laugh, and when I say laugh, I am not referring to some comedian. We are talking about friends here.

It does pay to have a lot of friends. It makes one's life richer. The best thing about friends is that you can be yourself with them. And they too can be themselves with you. And that means letting it all out. We must remember that apart from being the dutiful husband or wife, your spouse should be your best friend as well.

That is one mistake that most couples make. They tend to look upon their friends and their spouses as separate. While it is perfectly normal to have friends, your best friend should always be your husband or wife. It should be someone you can share your dreams and fears with, someone who understands, someone who can give your hand a gentle squeeze when things go wrong and someone who can brighten up your darkest day.

All this is a very far cry from sex, right? That is why we did mention earlier that looks and sex should be the last criteria in the selection of a life partner. The marriage proposal must come in a natural sequence, and it should by no means be the first thing that comes out as soon as you warm up to a person. You cannot very well say something like, "*Hey, you know what, I think we have the same tastes so let's get married.*"

You can say that of course but it would not be in very good taste. So, what do you do if you discover that one of the friends that you made and the one whom you were keeping your fingers crossed about is already married?

Do you have a car? Then the answer is simple, just run over that person's spouse and remove the unwanted element, right? Wrong! It is just not done. You can still be friends with that person and shift your attention towards another direction. Who knows, you might even find a better person. All you must do is shuffle your cards and deal them out again.

I hope you have got the hang of what we meant by working backwards now. There is another catch involved in this process. There is a chance that one of the friends that you made may have read this book too and maybe the proposal may come from the other end. If it does, then well and good; for it saves you the ritual.

Mr Right and Miss. Wrong

But then, what if the person who proposed to you wasn't really what you had in mind? Well, the choice is yours of course; you can take it or leave it. But there is a point worth considering here. If we can find someone that we love, that is good, but if we find someone who loves us, isn't that better?

But I would also like to add a word here. Suppose someone comes and proposes to you but you are not interested, you have every right to turn the proposal down. There is no need to hurt the other person's ego. However, if you know that you cannot marry this person, a turned-down proposal is better than a divorce. Try to explain your feelings in the gentlest way possible.

CHAPTER FOUR

Your Appearance and Profile

Nobody is perfect in this world but that does not mean that we cannot try to look our best. There is absolutely nothing wrong with giving nature a helping hand. Work on your image, work on your profile and work on your appearance.

Many people go by the philosophy, "*This is me, whether you like it or not it's your problem. I am not going to change.*" Well, nobody is asking you to change, but what are you trying to do? Scare people off? Well, the fact is, such statements are just a manifestation of your insecurity. We all have a certain degree of insecurity, some people more than others. It is this insecurity that makes us sound gruff and uncaring when it comes to improving our appearances.

Whatever you are afraid of, others are afraid of the same thing. In this world, most people are neither for us nor against us. They are thinking about themselves. Presenting oneself is an area that requires a lot of work, but surprisingly, this is the one area which people tend to neglect the most. Most of us have a laid-back attitude when it comes to painting a picture of ourselves. When it comes to presenting yourself, we have some work to do.

If we knew you on a more personal basis, we would have loved to help you to chalk out a profile of yourself that would be as impressive as possible. But of course, it is impossible to know all our readers on a one-to-one basis. But you do not have to worry because we have done a lot of study in this regard and once you follow our directions, you can indeed come up with that dream profile.

The Dream Profile

One cannot take too much effort into preparing a profile. It is something that should be viewed in all seriousness. Please do not treat the subject lightly. Imagine that you are preparing for a job; won't you spend a lot of time getting your resume ready?

Well, most of us take up jobs for how long, four or five years? And how about a relationship? We do not go into a relationship with the expectation that it would last for a couple of years. We have to understand that a relationship is worth much more than a job because it is probably the most important decision in life. So now let us discuss ways in which you can spruce up your profile.

You can of course get a professional to do the job for you since it saves you the effort. You may have to dish out a small amount, of course, but it could be worth it. Many people have qualms about including a picture in the profile. Well, I don't want to press the issue. It certainly does look better to have a picture in your profile, but due to privacy issues, you can refrain from including a picture.

The best thing you could do is once you are comfortable chatting with a person and are convinced that this person does not have any devious intentions, you could send your picture over as an attachment or a file. But this, too, is best done on a mutual exchange basis. It would be unfair if you know what the other person looks like but the other person is kept in the dark and vice versa.

The Face in the Mirror

Now, coming to the picture as such, if you are sending over a picture of yourself, for heaven's sake, send over a decent picture. It should be a recent one and please do not make any compromises about the quality. Get a professional to do the job for you and with the digital techniques of today, they can do a very impressive job. At the same time, do work on your expression before the photograph is taken. Stand in front of your mirror and try out various expressions till you get something that you think is the best for you. And remember that it has to be a picture of you smiling.

You should not have the classic hangdog expression or the "*butter-will-not-melt-in-my-mouth expression*". Smile, it costs you nothing and it lights up a person's face.

Now, the first thing that you should do is take out a pencil and paper and write down the raw details about yourself. By raw details, we are referring to things like your age, your height and your weight. This is the skeleton on which we are going to work on. And when we have added enough flesh and blood to this backbone, even you will be impressed by your profile! But first, let us steer clear of certain pitfalls into which most people fall.

The Modesty Pitfall

Most of us have been trained to be very modest. When it comes to saying something good about ourselves we feel very queasy about blowing our own trumpet. Right, nobody is asking you to do any trumpet blowing but facts have to be stated as facts.

If you are a music lover and have a good voice too, I can't see why you can't put it down like that. Why can't you declare simply without sounding very proud that you have a good voice? A pointer that you could bear in mind would be to add something like, "*My friends think that I sing rather well*".

There now, you can't feel too bad about something as simple as that. It is as good as saying "*Some people think that I sing well, but it is for you to decide whether I have a good voice or not.*" Similar statements that you can work on and even add are given below.

"*Lots of people appreciate my cooking.*"

"*I am no Rembrandt, but I enjoy painting.*"

"*I like decorating, and many of my friends think that my tastes are not too bad.*"

So go ahead, if you have a talent, you might as well let others know about it; after all, a talented person would like to be appreciated by a partner.

While we are talking about modesty, there is one question that I want to address right now. It is something that all of us are familiar with. If you have chatted with a stranger with whom you are trying to build a rapport, you must have been confronted with the question before. The question is "what do you look like?' I have often wondered about the sense of this question. The best answers that I could come up with are "*I look like a cross between an orangutan and a Tasmanian devil*" or "*I have my mother's teeth, my father's nose, my uncle's eyes and my roommates' shoes.*"

But of course, we cannot give such answers which, funny though they might sound, might just rub the person in the wrong way. What the person means is, "*Are you good-looking or not?*"

A very tricky question indeed! How can you answer such a question without sounding either super modest or extremely vain? The answer to that is not to tell them the answer directly. You can say something like:

"I am as fresh as peppermint."

"I look like a bunch of fresh lilies."

"I have the appeal of a bowl of fresh fruit."

If the person still does not take the hint, then give them a detailed description of every inch and let him or her decide for himself or herself.

The Braggart Pitfall

Bragging, as we all know, is a major turnoff. So it is best to steer completely clear of it. This is especially true in the case of physical attributes. You might be one hell of a looker, but let the other person decide, remember that what wine is for Peter can turn off to be venom for Paul.

You can make implied statements like, "*I am certainly not a bad looker*," or "*Opinion is divided, some people think that I am good-looking while others think that I am not.*" But perhaps the best way of describing yourself would be to add a touch of humour to it.

If you are chubby you could say something like, "*I am round in all the right places...I hope.*" If you are tall you could say something like, "*Some say I should play basketball.*" If you are on the short side you could say something like, "*I might seem to be lacking in size but I assure you, it is all there.*"

Do you know the best part about such witty remarks about oneself? Humour always works. All of us have been blessed with a sense of humour to some degree at least and if a person can make funny comments about himself or herself, that always acts as a turn-on. And you can take my word for it; humour sells like a billion dollars.

The Hackneyed Pitfall

We have seen and heard other people describe themselves and these kinds of descriptions sort of sink into our heads. The moment someone asks us to describe ourselves, we start by using hackneyed phrases.

I think it is much better to completely steer clear of hackneyed phrases. It makes us look like just another face in the crowd. Tell me, unless you have an identical twin, have you ever seen anyone who looks exactly like you? Then why should your description of yourself sound like a banal organ that has been played again and again? Try to sound as original as you can. Make yourself sound interesting. Try to use as many similes and comparisons as possible. If you are blonde, well don't just say that you are blonde. You could use descriptions like, "*My hair is the colour of freshly harvested hay.*"

If you are a brunette, you could say something like: "*My hair colour would make a raven blush." If you have red hair, you could try something like, "My hair is like the setting sun.*"

Another point that I would like to add is that you do not have to belittle yourself. Every coin has two sides and it all depends on the way you look at it. For example, if you have dark skin, there is no reason to feel bad about it. It all depends on how you put it across. You could try expressions like, "*If you like chocolate then you are going to love the colour of my skin.*" Or "*My body looks like polished wood.*"

Remember, beauty lies in the eyes of the beholder, and it is left to you to convince the beholder. Most people are willing to believe what you tell them, provided you tell them convincingly enough.

The Boredom Pitfall

Try to make yourself sound as interesting as possible. I mean it. If you are painting a self-portrait, you might as well use the right colours. Before we leave our homes what do we do? We all spend at least five minutes in front of our mirrors in an attempt to make ourselves look as presentable and as impressive as possible.

Well, the same thing applies to our profile. Remove all drab details about yourself that might be of no interest to the reader. If your job is something like *editing journals on the etymology of words derived from ancient Aramaic*, well, just say that you have an editing job.

Similarly, try to bear in mind that anything can be put down in two ways. You can either make it interesting or boring; so work on it until you are sure that it will not bore a reader to death and the best test for this would be to hand it over to a close friend and ask that friend's opinion. Nobody likes a bore so take all efforts not to sound like one.

The Vagueness Pitfall

At the same time, whatever you put down about yourself must not be confusing. It just does not work to put down a statement like, "*While I am not given to sports, nor am I considered to be an outdoor person, I have developed a passing interest in watching football, and have had my stints with Terra firma.*" If anything drives people away, statements like this certainly do. For Heaven's sake avoid phrases like "*I am different,*" especially when you are talking about your appearance. The other person will in all likelihood conjure up images of a three-horned monster or a lion-tailed monkey.

Another example is when you use phrases like, "*I don't play by the rules,*" or "*I am game for something new.*" These expressions can be hopelessly misleading and it is the easiest thing in the world to add a sexual innuendo to such an expression and that would be a sure-shot method of biting off more than you can chew.

Now that we have discussed the major pitfalls, let us go to the real profile. The reason I said real profile is that the profile must indeed reflect the person you are.

The Web of Deceit

While you might take some care to conceal your identity it is best not to lie. Do not try to bluff your way through a relationship because at some time the whole thing might come out and as we all know, one lie leads to another and then before you know it the whole relationship will crash. Be as honest and as frank as you can, taking care to conceal your identity.

Someone once said that a friend is someone who knows all about you and loves you just the same. So there is no need to hide things about yourself. Of course, you do not have to tell the person every ghastly, gory detail about yourself, but at the same time, you do not have to conjure up stuff about yourself that just is not true. If at all you do paint a very rosy picture about yourself, including things that just are not true, or are far-fetched exaggerations, and the other person does flip for you, in reality, you will be basking in another person's glory. This picture you have painted is just not you.

Your Alter Ego!

When you choose a handle to identify yourself by, you have to be sharp. Do not try to attract as many partners as possible. After all, what are we looking for, quality or quantity? Try to attract only the kind of people you are interested in and who would find you interesting. That is why we suggested that you use a handle that better defines the kind of person you are. Do not try to sound like a sex god or a sex goddess. If you are, let the other person decide for himself or herself; (it is much better than having the person come up with statements like "*Is it in yet?*") So steer clear of handles like Megastud, Handsomehunk, Superbabe or Bedlover.

Instead of that, you could try handles that give one an immediate idea about the kind of person you are. If you are an outdoor person use something like Natureguy or Naturegirl; if you are a music freak use something like Musicman or Musicmaid. If you are into theatre and stuff like that you could choose a name like Theatreguy or Theatregirl.

The point is to win over people who are interested in the same stuff as you are. That of course increases your chances of gelling with the person.

Brevity is Key!

Another crucial thing about writing your profile is that you should keep it as brief as possible. Nobody and that means nobody wants to read through lines and lines of another person's profile.

If you make it so long-winded, the person who is reading it will get the idea that you are the kind of person who would love to keep on talking about yourself, and instead of going on a date with you, the reader would rather curl up and die. But that doesn't mean that you have to limit the whole thing to just a few words. A too-brief profile would sound as if you do not have time for all this, but you are just doing it for the heck of it.

The best style that you could use would be to be 100% natural. Write your profile as you would describe yourself to a person directly. The conversation style has the widest appeal I might add. Make it simple and stay away from big words and hackneyed expressions.

You are Unique!

Think about it for a minute. Look at yourself in the mirror. Do you look like anyone else that you know? We all look so different though essentially we have been endowed with the same external characteristics, which are one nose, one mouth, two eyes and two ears.

So, despite having the same building blocks, if we can look so different why do we have to sound alike? Think about yourself differently. Do not just consider your likes and dislikes when you are writing your profile, consider your endearing qualities as well. Endearing qualities, what are those? Those are those qualities which make you liked by others. Of course, these are things that we never bother about but maybe we should. So what I would suggest would be to ask your best friends why they like you. Who knows, their answers just might surprise you! But at least you will get an idea of what you can include in your profile.

You could try out the following exercise to find out what kind of a person you are. I won't say that the results are foolproof but they certainly might be interesting.

The Animal Test

Which among the following animals do you identify with most?

A shark

A rabbit

A bear

A hen

A dog

A cat

If you chose a shark, you are generally an aggressive kind of person who has no time for others who are not up to the mark. You won't think twice about slicing through those who stand in your way and you have a very clear idea about what you want and you know how to get it too.

If you chose a rabbit, you are generally sweet-tempered but timid. You bend very easily. You like to stay clear from the limelight as far as possible and not interfere much in the affairs of others.

If you chose the bear, you are a warm person by nature but not very sure about whether others like you. Hence you might go out of your way to win friends and love reassuring others.

If you chose the hen, then you are one of those people who constantly fuss about minor details. You keep your eyes open but you are very dependable, though sometimes you might end up poking your nose into things that do not concern you.

If you chose the dog, you are a happy-go-lucky person. You are willing to help others but if you do not watch out, more than once you might be taken for a ride. You do not bother about trifles but when you lose your head, it is lost.

If you chose the cat, you live in a world of your own; you do not trouble others and do not like others troubling you. In short, you are very much the modern apartment creature who knows all the manners but uses them only to be civil.

Now, the descriptions given here are just general guidelines but I suppose that it does give you a cue about how to write your profile. You can do it by yourself. Think about the animal or bird that you like best. Do not consider physical attributes but think of traits or characteristics that you like.

Then you can sit down and write a brief description about the animal and hey presto! Before you even know it, your profile is ready but it would be a good idea to delete the name of the animal when you post your profile.

There is something that I want all my readers to understand. Each one of us has something remarkable about us. It is all a question of finding out what those qualities are. Do not always believe what other people have to say about you. Don't you have something to say about yourself?

Pretend as if you were talking to your best friend. Talk to yourself. If your best friend were to ask you what his or her endearing qualities are, then wouldn't you be quick to reassure the person? Well, the same thing applies to you as well. You can be your own best friend. And when you try out this exercise on yourself, well, you have a list of your plus points ready. If you can do this for your friend, then you can do it for yourself as well.

Such an exercise is very useful not just from the dating point of view, but only if we understand what our positive traits are, can we understand what kind of a person we deserve to get. The same holds about our negative traits too, but then nobody is perfect.

CHAPTER FIVE

Letting the Relationship Blossom

Right, so now we are as ready as we can be with our interests all chalked out and our profiles posted. It is a perfect picture. It is almost like being seated alone at this posh restaurant, dressed to kill, with a glass of champagne in one hand and the other hand swung over the back of the chair. You have a smile on your lips, a twinkle in your eye and an invitation on your face.

So what happens next? This person who appears to be the perfect match for you catches your eye and saunters towards you. Now, what do you do? Please remember that the description above was about a virtual environment. In effect, what we meant is that while you spend time idling in a chat room, this is the mood that you are going to generate.

So what happens when a person takes the cue and starts chatting? Well, that is an intelligent question. I would like to make one thing clear here. The Internet is like any other highway. It is not safe until you get to know your way around. So what I would suggest would be to trust your instincts and proceed with caution. You can sound like a very warm person but please be extremely cautious about giving out any personal information.

Nicknames and Pet names

Let the other person know that you would prefer to be known by the handle you use or even better, you could tell the person to call you a pet name but let the person know that it is indeed a pet name, because at a later date, if the relationship blossoms it doesn't look nice if you have to say something like, "*Gee, I'm sorry, but my name isn't Janice, it is Heptullah, I guess I lied to you.*"

The best thing, in this case, would be to let yourself be known by the name of some celebrity. You could call yourself Cinderella or Pocahontas or Archie, Betty or Veronica. The chatting has now begun and you can start exchanging information. Keep to the general and stay away from the specific.

Helping your Memory

The human brain is indeed a remarkable thing. It is capable of storing and processing such a wide range of information that even a supercomputer would shy away when compared to it. But due to the virtual explosion of information, our memories have become very selective.

This means that we cannot recollect everything that we hear or see. Do not trust your memory too much when it comes to chatting over the net. You might meet a lot of people over the net and you might chat with a couple of them. So eventually it might become difficult to remember all of them and their details as well. Or even worse than that is that you might become confused and mix up details. It would look bad for you if you call a person the wrong name, or ask the person the wrong details. In such cases where you have been chatting with many persons, for heaven's sake jot down the details about each person separately or create separate files for each person and store them on your computer.

When you add them to your friends list, use handles or nicknames that can help you remember the person the moment you start chatting at a later date. Now, in case you do not remember the person, then it is inadvisable to play the guessing game. The other person might get very offended if you say something like, "Is it Sarah or Mary?"

In such cases when you have a genuine lapse of memory, the best thing to do is, to be honest with the person and say, "I know we chatted the other day, but I'm sorry, can you please refresh my memory about you?"

Small Talk

Few topics are best for the initial talks so that intimacy is not developed and at the same time, you do not have to struggle for matters of common interest. You can talk about the weather, sports, movies, music and even food.

But at the same, it is in bad taste to discuss religion, politics and family matters in the initial stages. You can crack jokes but dirty jokes are an absolute no-no at least in the first few talks.

Once you have talked more than once or twice and you feel comfortable with the person, you can give the person your e-mail address but remember this is the first step towards virtual intimacy so you have to trust your instincts and nothing else. This takes things out of the public chat rooms and into the private inboxes.

Beware of Instant Intimacy

Many people feel that e-mail will never have the warmth or the personal touch of the old-fashioned letters and cards that people used to send through the postal service. That may be true but e-mail has an advantage of the here and the now.

Because you are aware of the fact that the person you are chatting with is reaching out to you in the same way as you are reaching out to that person, there is a tendency for intimacy to build up even before you know it.

The medium ceases to be the deciding factor and when a person presses you for information which you have to supply immediately, you might let certain details slip out unless you are well prepared. You have to be on your guard all the time and keep constantly reminding yourself that the person you are chatting with is, after all, a stranger and a goodness-knows-what. The best thing that you could do is avoid instant intimacy altogether.

It doesn't matter if the other person finds you cold or reserved, you can easily solve that by telling the other person that it takes some time for you to become comfortable with a person. That is a good quality because it is as good as saying, "Well, I'm sorry I'm not the loose kind who plays around."

There is something that many of my readers might want to know and that is how to find out if the other person is lying. As I had told you earlier, the Net can be a very unsafe place and so we have to be sure about the good faith of the other person before revealing any personal details about ourselves. So the next part has been devoted specifically to that.

How to Tell If Someone Is Lying

As discussed earlier, we are not going to resort to singles' chat rooms dedicated specifically to online dating. Instead, we will be in chat rooms of specific interest. So one very effective way of finding out if a person is lying would be to ask the person very pointed questions about the area of interest. If the person fumbles or gives vague answers then you do not have to waste your time on such a person.

Another thing that you could do is, from the moment you first make contact, jot down whatever details the person chooses to reveal to you and in subsequent encounters nonchalantly question the person about the details, if there is a contradiction in the two details then you can be as sure as pat that the person is lying.

Ask the person seemingly general questions which in fact should have a very definite purpose, for example, ask the person what he or she is looking for in such a relationship. Note down the answer. After two or three encounters again repeat the question and see whether the two answers match.

You could try pretending that you have chatted with the person before and innocently ask the person if he or she is the person (make something up) and try offering compliments to the person like, "I enjoyed chatting with you the other day. You were perfectly charming..." and so on. If the person falls for cheap flattery like this, then obviously he or she makes it a hobby to chat with people under various identities.

And so the chatting goes on until the person grows on you. When you feel that you can trust the person, you may try giving the person your telephone number. Remember that this too is a giant leap towards building a relationship so it's better that you be sure than sorry.

The safest thing you can do about telephone numbers is to mutually exchange them preferably at the same time so that neither party is at a disadvantage. It's no big deal, you can afford to tell the person that you are just being wary, and the person will understand. If he or she does not, then there is a good chance that he or she will not understand a lot of other things as well. In that case, dump the person.

CHAPTER SIX

Meeting Face to Face

Once you have started talking over the telephone, then the relationship has already taken wings; then there is no reason to postpone a direct meeting. So, what are you waiting for? But wait; there is no need to push it. You should not sound over-anxious to meet this girl or guy. Let the decision to meet evolve over several telephone calls. And there are certain things that you can bear in mind before you meet.

The Rendezvous

It is not advisable to invite someone home before you have met the person. You had better choose a public place preferably somewhere where there are plenty of people around, just in case, you know. That is why most couples prefer to meet in a restaurant over lunch or dinner. There is one thing about having food together. When people sit together and have food together they get to know a lot about each other.

Table manners tell us a lot about a person's upbringing and background and you can learn a lot about a person by observing him or her eat. The second thing is that warm food has a wonderful effect on the human mind. It releases all those digestive juices and sets the tongue wagging. People loosen up a lot, especially after a glass of wine or two.

The first mistake that most people make is that they go under the wrong impression that a meeting, even the first meeting must end up in bed. No, it does not have to be so.

There is no compulsion on your part or anyone's part that you have to take the person home with you. Just because you enjoy talking or chatting with a person does not necessarily mean that you have to sleep with the person. Let that too evolve, so it is best to keep any such situations that might lead to a bedroom scene completely at bay.

So how do you do that? The first thing you should do is you should be clear about the time. Evenings are tricky times to meet. If you have dinner together, then there comes the possibility of dropping the other person home. And of course, you can't just accept a ride and walk away after being dropped off without inviting the other person in. And then one thing will lead to the other and then the inevitable is bound to happen. Of course, if that's the way you would like it to be, then you just have to do what I just told you not to do.

Lunchtime is the best time because in the daytime most of us are busy with work and we can just spare an hour or a half for lunch. So you can always leave on the pretext that you have to get back to work or something like that. Very few people end up going home together after lunch. Another thing is that at lunch the element of romance does not come in.

Take care to be at the arranged spot on time, you certainly do not want to keep a person you are meeting for the first time waiting. Dress appropriately for the occasion, and keep it simple but at the same time, it should be something that looks good on you.

Leaving Your Mark Behind

Now, suppose this date did work out as planned and you really and thoroughly enjoyed the company of the other person, you would want the other person to remember you and think about you, wouldn't you? So how do you make sure that the other person does think about you? The answer is simple. Just leave your mark behind. Mind you, a business or visiting card is not appropriate here. It lends a very formal colour to the picture. Surely you do not want the person to remember you for your credentials or your designation. Something more personalized would be more appropriate.

Put your artistic and creative talents into full gear. If you are poetic, you could pen down a few lines on a small card and hand it to the person. Mind you, the lines should not be about the person, but about general topics like friendship, relationships, togetherness, warmth, or meetings. But do the writing in advance and keep it for the right moment. Do not try to write a poem on a paper napkin with the person sitting in front of you!

If you can't write poetry, maybe you could get some dried flowers and stick them onto a card and copy down the lines of somebody else, but admit that the lines are not yours to the person. Keep such a token with you and wait for the right moment. Just before you part, if you are sure that "*this is the one*" then hand it over to the person with a very shy expression on your face and a timid, "*I made this for you...*" Believe me, it is miles better to say "I made this for you" than "*I bought this for you*".

So, what happens if you are not too sure that you want to see this person again? Well, keep it with you and save it for the next person. If the person is the right person, and if you did hand the person this personalized token, the person is sure to think of you in a much fonder way.

Clothes Make a Man (Or Woman)

You do not have to be dressed to kill when you go out for lunch. The best thing about lunch dates is that most of us would be in our work clothes and that saves us the agony of choosing the right thing to wear on a first date.

A wonderful thing that you could do when going on a first date is to make it a group activity, preferably a foursome. This takes away the awkwardness of the situation and takes away all those embarrassing moments of silence.

A group has another advantage in that lesser attention will be focused on each other so that there is less stress and as a result, both partners would be more relaxed. It is also safer too since there is safety in numbers. But the company to be included should be mutually agreeable and not be thrust upon the other person. But take care to avoid any person whom you know to be a chatterbox; it takes all the fun away if one person dominates the conversation.

You may drink if you want to, but do not drink too much on your first date. Not only is it in bad taste but when you are drunk, you might blurt out something which you didn't mean to and that might ruin everything.

Footing the Bill

It is a good idea to decide beforehand and communicate your decision to go Dutch, which means that each person should pay for whatever he or she has. That's the way that it is supposed to be because if nothing works out of this relationship you certainly do not want to be obliged to the person.

When you choose the place, avoid secluded spots and places that you are not familiar with. But the ambience is indeed important. You cannot expect to have a tête-à-tête in a crowded shopping mall, can you?

Many Dates

So, what happens if you get more than one offer to date at the same time? Or in other words, what happens if you become close to more than one person at a time? Hey, that is probably the very thing we are looking out for. You could go on different dates and then compare for yourself and choose the best person.

You do not have to leap for the first person who caught your fancy. You have the right to choose, so go ahead and do it. There is no need to feel guilty about two-timing anybody as long as you do not promise anyone that you are not seeing anyone else.

And what happens if you bump into date number one while you are out with date number 2? Well, all you have to do is treat it as the most natural thing in the world. Introduce date No.1 to date No. 2 as your friends and watch how they behave. This is an excellent way of finding out how a jealous husband or wife may behave in future.

But whatever happens, a double date, that is going out with two people together is completely out of the question!

CHAPTER SEVEN

Meeting Your Date Physically

When you are dating online, you have a lot of things to your advantage. For example, the other person does not see you and you do not have to bother about appearances. You can devote your entire energy towards sounding intelligent and witty.

But when you are seated in front of a person, there are a thousand things that you have to pay attention to. Many people believe that it is not important to keep up appearances. They feel that it is more important to be oneself. It sounds good enough. But on your first date at least, you certainly have to keep up appearances. The other person should not feel ashamed to be seen around with you and so you should try as hard as possible to avoid that *faux pas*.

Let us start with your physical appearance. I mentioned earlier that you do not have to dress to kill, however, you must appear well-groomed. Take special care of things like nails, hair, and teeth. Check for bad breath too because that indeed is the worst turn-off.

What you wear should not be loud and attract the wrong kind of attention. Choose something that you are comfortable in and at the same time that looks good on you. Ladies, please be careful about your make-up, and remember that make-up is meant to accentuate your looks not to hide them. It is best to avoid garish colours.

You should smell good of course but don't overdo it. We certainly don't want you to remain in the other person's memory as just one strong smell. Men, please take care to go in for masculine scents like musk, or smells from nature. Women, keep it as light and dainty as possible.

The Secret is Charm

All the things that have been said so far are about how you can create a favourable impression. There is something that is equally or even more important than that, and that is to make the other person feel comfortable. Help the other person relax.

Anyway, you have been chatting for quite some time, so you do know a great deal about each other. The best thing you can do is to ease the tension and break the ice. Sometimes the ice gets so thick that you can feel it. Break it up by cracking a joke or two. But the joke should be spontaneous and in keeping with the situation or else it will fall flat. Do not rehearse a joke because a rehearsed joke sounds well rehearsed.

The key word here is *charm*. Use all the charm that you can muster. Try to be as considerate and as thoughtful as possible. Do not dominate the conversation but try to get the other person talking. People generally love to talk about themselves so try to get the other person talking by asking about the person's work. Show interest in whatever the other person says.

Try to be a good conversationalist. A good conversationalist is not a person who talks well but one who listens well also. So try to be a good listener. And while you are listening try not to get distracted by something else or the other person might feel that you are losing interest in what he or she is saying.

Then comes the question, "What do you do if you find that the other person is dominating the conversation?" Well, in that case, listen patiently for a minute or two and then give a subtle sign like a raised eyebrow or a smile through the corner of your mouth. If the other person is intelligent enough, he or she will get the cue. If not, then take your chance, you might have to listen to this person for the rest of your life.

Humour rarely fails. But again take care not to overdo it. There is only one thing worse than a total lack of humour and that is too much humour.

Gifts

It is a good idea to take a gift along with you as that does create a good impression, but remember that when you are courting the gifts should be limited to flowers or chocolates only. While you are chatting try to find out what the other person likes in flowers and chocolates. You certainly don't want to give the person flowers that he or she is allergic to.

The object of your gift should not be to woo the person but to create a good and lasting impression. There is no sense in splurging a lot on your first date for there is no rule that everything should work out well the first time. Do not overdo it and at the same time do not appear cheap and stingy either.

However, if the other person has forgotten to bring you a gift, be quick to reassure the person that it is perfectly alright. Do not let the other person feel uneasy. That is a wonderful way to make the conversation light. You can jokingly tell the other person to get you a gift the next time.

ONLINE DATING FOR SENIOR CITIZENS

CHAPTER EIGHT

Technically, a person is considered a senior citizen when they reach the age of 65. However, that's not always the way the public feels – especially those who have hit the age of 50. To some people, this might send them into spasms of denial. After all, how can you be 60 when you still feel 30 in your mind? But that's a good way to think. It's been said many, many times that age is simply a number – it's a state of mind about how old you are!

If you're over 50 years old, you've likely heard many times by now that you're over the hill. What started this rumour that once you've reached the middle of your life, it's all downhill from there?

Today's baby boomers will stop at nothing to put an end to this rumour. They'll prove that the over-50 crowd is stronger and smarter than ever. Those over age 50 are more physically active than ever. Many have a decent amount of disposable income. They are politically active, culturally motivated and in tune with modern trends.

Mark Twain once said "Age is an issue of mind over matter. If you don't mind, it doesn't matter." Truer words, I think, have never been spoken! So you're a senior citizen – so what! Life doesn't have to be relegated to planting flowers and rocking on your front porch talking about the good old days. Believe me; the good old days are just starting!

With maturity comes new knowledge and experiences that you can embrace and enjoy. You are blessed with the memories you can share with those around you – your loved ones. But what if you're a single senior? Is all hope lost for sharing your life and those memories with someone else? Not a chance!

Many of those over the age of 50 actively date. Loss of a spouse or partner due to death or divorce or other life situation is no longer the beginning of many lonely years spent in mourning. Instead, dating for the over-50 crowd is big business.

At one time, dating for seniors was essentially unthought-of. The consensus "back in the day" was that you found someone to marry and stayed married to them forever. Once they passed away, you were expected to simply live out the rest of your days as a widow or widower. Well, the times have changed.

Divorce can also bring you to a new single status. The divorce rate today is alarmingly high, but for some people, there just isn't another option.

Studies have shown that staying single can also put your health at risk. Researchers from the University of Chicago and Duke University have found that the longer a man spends in a divorced or widower state:

- The higher his likelihood of developing heart or lung disease or cancer
- The greater his risk of high blood pressure, diabetes, and stroke
- The more difficulties he will have with mobility, such as walking or climbing stairs

This particular study only involved men, but we're willing to be that women run those same risks as well. It makes sense then to get back out in the social scene and date – for your health!

If you're over 50 and you'd like to date, put your fears aside. There are so many safe ways to meet others who are in a similar situation. No longer do those over 50 have to rely on friends or family or neighbours to provide them with dating opportunities.

Why should you be expected to be alone when you still have so much life to live? You shouldn't! So you need to get out there and meet people – date, have fun, make new memories, and have new experiences! What's the best way to do that?

At one time, the only places to meet people were at church, in the grocery store, or through family and friends. Today, we have the Internet and you should take advantage of everything it has to offer in your journey back into the dating world.

Meeting new people can be challenging at any age, but for the senior, it can be especially daunting. If you've spent years with one person, you may not know where to begin. We think that's normal, but don't worry.

A quick search on the Internet shows there are many, many websites dedicated to dating for the senior set. But it can be daunting – especially for those who aren't Internet savvy. That's where we come in!

We can't teach you the ins and outs of the Internet, but we're betting since you've bought this book, you already are somewhat computer-literate. You don't have to know everything about the Internet to start dating online. You just need to know how to log on.

Inside this book, you'll find everything you need to know to get started in the online dating scene. We'll give you all kinds of tips and tricks on how to create your online profile, what to look for in a potential date, and ways to keep yourself safe.

CHAPTER NINE

Should You Date Online as a Senior?

Online dating isn't just for young people. We've told you that today there are many, many places online for vibrant, enthusiastic seniors to meet people. They all offer different services and provide features that you may or may not like. But in general, online dating can be a very positive experience for a single senior.

With an online dating service, there are lots of choices. Not since high school or college will you find such a large number of potential dates and mates in one place. It can be heartening just to know that there are many single seniors out there who would love to find a loving partner.

Since there are so many people on the Internet dating scene, it should be enough proof that it does work, right? Some people are a little iffy about putting themselves out to strangers, but with the advancing technology making the world smaller and smaller every day, the word 'stranger' sometimes means nothing anymore.

Online dating sites give you a wide list of people to choose from. You can choose them because you have shared interests, belong to the same city, or whatever. And because dating sites have this vast list, you have the liberty to skip and choose. This erases having to care for a few caterpillars before you reach butterflies if you know what I mean.

Dating sites cater to different needs. Some focus on letting single women meet single men. Some filter according to sexuality, religion, sex, or race -- the possibilities are endless. You name it; you bet there is something or someone out there who will fit just perfectly with what you're looking for.

The key to getting the most out of your online dating site membership is to know what you want and what you're looking for, so you won't waste time trying to get to know people who turn out to be at the polar end of your character spectrum. Don't join a matchmaking site if you're just after the date's "fun" side. Don't join a Catholic site if you're Jewish. Things like that.

It's relatively inexpensive. While there are many free chat rooms and online personal sites, you may want to invest in paying a small fee to meet people who are more serious about meeting a quality partner. Even if you pay $25 to $50 to join, it's still cheaper than a senior cruise, and you don't have to leave home.

Profiles are a fun way to learn about people. Sites that offer space to write personal profiles that include hobbies, special interests, political beliefs, dreams, goals and favourite activities will give you the most accurate idea of what a person is like, and will help you decide if you have enough in common to make a connection.

It's easy to connect. By exchanging emails, you get to know each other slowly, without the awkwardness that comes with first dates. If you choose to meet, you'll already know a lot about each other, and that could help you both feel more comfortable.

There are, however, downfalls to dating online. Some sites allow people to post their profiles and respond to others for free, but unfortunately, these free sites often attract weirdoes or perverts. It's important to check out the site carefully before you join.

Plus, it can be risky when it comes to the people you will meet. After all, there are people out there who lie. You need to be cautious. To get more responses, or in some cases to deliberately mislead, some people lie in their profiles. Don't believe everything you read – if he or she sounds too good to be true, he or she probably is.

Overall, however, many people have found true love through online dating services. You shouldn't have to spend the rest of your life alone. You deserve to live your life! There are people out there waiting to meet you. It's time for you to get started!

CHAPTER TEN

Now That You Are Online

You'll want to check the site often – every day if possible – ideally several times per day. People who have browsed through the site and seen your profile will send you communication that you can respond to if you choose. This is usually done with the site's system instead of through email. You may receive someone's email address to reply to and it's up to you whether or not you give them yours. You may want to hold off on that initially, however, avoiding being spammed and possibly harassed.

You can also browse through who is available out there that might interest you. If you find someone you like, send them an instant message and see what happens. The website will usually send you several possible matches for you each day. Check your e-mail and log onto the site faithfully. If anyone catches your eye, respond to them. Be proactive, not reactive. After all, you're online to find a date – don't let a chance pass you by!

The great thing about online dating services is that participants get to choose the persons they're going to communicate with. Plus, they get to read their profiles ahead of time, so they would have an idea about what type of a person they are dealing with before they make contact.

As connections are made, members of online dating services are free to correspond back and forth with the other members, at a pace that makes them comfortable. There's no need to feel pressured into setting up an in-person date until both members feel comfortable doing so.

When you are communicating with someone, there are a few things to keep in mind. You want to be as careful as possible in the early stages of your foray into internet dating. We can't say this strongly enough – never divulge personal information online in any circumstances unless you are fully and completely sure that the person on the other end is truthful and trustworthy.

Any pieces of information you provide could be used against you. Especially concerning financial aspects, do not easily give your trust to a person you meet online and give him your bank account number, electronic PINs and the like. While that may seem like simple common sense, you'd be surprised at how many people do this!

You should immediately cease communicating with someone obsessed with obtaining your personal information. All you need to do is tell the other person you're not comfortable yet telling them about that. If they persist, stop communicating with them.

If your purpose is only to exchange ideas with another person, share your experiences and beliefs. You don't have to give details about yourself if they insist. And even if your purpose is to find a date, don't give in too quickly by telling everything about yourself. Besides, you can test a person's sincerity when they value your decisions and listen to what you say.

Talk about things you might have in common. Initially, keep these conversations toward interests and hobbies.

Avoid talking specifically about children, grandchildren, etc. Be vague about jobs and locations until a trust can be established.

Remember that what you see is not always what you get when it comes to online dating services. Photos can easily be manipulated so the person you see in the photo may not resemble the person when it comes time to meet face-to-face. Sometimes people post photos taken many years ago so you see a much younger-looking person than you're likely to encounter.

Words can lie, too. Someone might post the most impressive profile as a way of getting a lot of connections, but in the end fail to live up to the lifestyle that is presented in the profile. So, when pursuing the dating scene on the Internet, proceed with caution. If this method of dating does not sound like a good idea to you, then try some of the other senior dating alternatives.

Always keep your eyes open to signs of fraud, cheating or obscenity. Don't get too engrossed by sweet nothings or mesmerized by good looks (as seen in the webcam or photo). Watch out if the person can keep their story straight and consistent. If they repeatedly inject sex into your conversations and are too demanding for private information or things that you are not at ease with talking about, end the conversation.

Don't be afraid to ask questions. It's perfectly normal to inquire about marital status, children, hopes, dreams, etc. If someone is uncomfortable with these questions, it's a good indication they have something to hide.

Find someone who shares your common interests, life goals and family preferences. It is important to share some of the same hopes for a relationship to be worthwhile.

During casual conversations, look for possible warning signs of control, jealousy or tempers. If an individual seems to be extremely needy or needs to talk to you every minute, this may be a sign of possessive behaviour and should be recognized early. If you notice this happening, move on and find another possible online dating match.

Don't rush. Take the time to get to know someone before you decide that you are comfortable enough to meet them. A relationship takes time to build and there is no reason to rush into anything.

If you learn that someone hasn't been honest about his/her profile or other detail, end the dating potential immediately. Dishonesty is no way to begin a relationship and it makes you question anything else that he/she may be hiding.

Be yourself. Don't pretend to like something or be someone that you are not just to please the other person. If they are the right one for you, there will not be a reason to pretend.

Don't be afraid to play the field. There are hundreds of possible matches out there for you – don't limit yourself to just one. Just as long as you're being honest and having fun, it's okay to keep contacting as many people as you like until you find someone you're interested in. After all, meeting new people is what dating is all about.

Reply to anyone who contacts you whether it is to say "Yes, I'm interested" or "I can't talk to you at this time". The generally accepted practice is to respond within one week. But remember that you may be turning down the right person, so you may want to just chat a little bit and see what happens!

In email communications, don't send out "form letters" to everyone. Don't make them sound like a business letter, be casual and conversational as you address something showing about them in their profile.

Do not just chat online. An electronic chat doesn't always suffice. Do phone conversations with him or her, as these would show social and communication skills. Avoid calling at home. Try calling from a cell phone or a telephone booth. Only when you are completely comfortable should you give your home number.

Exercise caution and common sense during these communications. Don't trust too easily, but don't get obsessive and think that everyone is lying. There are some tell-tale signs that people aren't being honest with you.

We think it's important to point out different things about online dating that aren't exactly positive. There are things you need to be aware of when you begin chatting with them.

Dangers and Precautions

Thousands of people have dated successfully online. However online dating sites are far from dating havens. There is a touch of hell that you must know about. Sad but true it is not a perfect world.

Some people submit profiles that are a bunch of lies. They hide facts and present an illusion that is very far from the truth. When you select a profile for a date try and discover the "actual" person beneath the layers.

Scammers abound, extremely charming and friendly there are online daters who will wrench details of your bank accounts out of you and poof the next day you will find your accounts wiped out. Never reveal important information over the net or personally unless you know for certain that x, y, or z is trustworthy.

Sadly the net is an open book and a person can easily find out your address and so on. Unscrupulous men and women can use the net and land on your doorstep endangering you and your family. Always use the e-mail facility provided by the site or an anonymous account. Never use personal e-mail accounts or e-mails belonging to the place of work.

Spammers use online dating sites to flood people with spam mail. Never reveal contact information just because the anonymous dater asked sweetly. Stalkers, rapists, and murderers can easily use the anonymity provided by online sites to find their next victim. Be wise follow safety rules and listen to your gut instincts.

Online dating sites are even used by cons and drug dealers. The sites do have security measures in place but have no way of verifying everything. So don't jump into a relationship in a hurry. Keep it friendly and casual until you know for certain that the person you find attractive is just an ordinary person like you.

The handsome hulk or buxom blond maybe just a celluloid image and the real person may look quite different and ordinary. So, never choose a person just on what they look like in the photo presented along with the profile. Look for substance in your conversations and communications.

Be aware as well that photos can be manipulated or altered. People might also use older photos that no longer resemble what they look like today. Yet another reason not to discount or fall for people is based solely on their photos. Many are just there for a one-night stand or fling. They use the sites as a playing field. Be alert that these types generally betray themselves through inconsistent behaviours.

You should also be aware that often married people will be online looking to cheat. Unless you're comfortable being the “other woman” or “other man”, which we’re pretty sure you’re not, these people should be avoided. You can get a sense of whether or not they’re married just from talking with them.

Don’t let the above turn you away from dating. Read these suggestions and be wise to know how to shift the pearls from the pebbles. Thousands of men and women have dated successfully using online sites. Don’t let the dangers scare you away.

CHAPTER ELEVEN

Online Flirting

Online dating is an excellent way of meeting new people and expanding your dating pool. For some, it is also a great way for getting back on the dating scene again. Though online dating sites are often stereotyped as an arena for the desperate, they are an effective venue for singles that are interested in meeting interesting people.

Most people who engage in online dating are those who lead busy lives and do not have time to indulge in time-demanding social activities. Others turn to online dating to widen their social horizons or simply to have a fresh start. But whatever their reasons, online dating is a proven way for social renewal.

Dating, in general, and in whatever venue, always goes hand in hand with flirting. For those who wonder if they can master the art of online flirting, of course, you can! All you need to do is learn all about the different online flirting approaches, and you are on your way to a successful online dating experience.

Online dating is usually carried on through live chat or electronic mail. In your communications, always keep it short, simple and sweet. Stick to light-hearted and upbeat tones in your conversations. This is proven to attract online dates. Use easy-to-answer questions, and in return make your responses simple in your e-mails.

In writing correspondence, always use screen names. Do not abuse "emoticons" such as :) and the likes. Emoticons may also be annoying when overdone or may sound too giddy or insincere. We'll address certain emoticons and lingo you might see online at the end of the book.

Use humour as your ally. Universally, humour is considered sexy. Try it, but of course, remember to use them in good taste. Deliver with confidence; dates will pick that up.

Compliment your date. Everyone likes to be complimented. The best compliments are those with the element of surprise. Keep your compliments sincere, honest, and genuine. And when you receive a compliment yourself, the best response would be to simply say, "Thank You!"

A great online flirting tip is to use "enticers" in your e-mail communications. You may want to try the tried and tested pick-up lines or devise your own. Try to keep them light and inviting so as not to sound predatory. The key is to sound cute, interested and above all sincere. This will help ignite a spark in your emails and will surely get you that much-coveted first date.

This may not seem to feel comfortable to you, but remember, you're just a name and a face and what you're saying is typed words on a screen. And don't overdo it. Avoid being overly suggestive and making too many sexual comments. You may be opening yourself up to something you're not prepared for.

Simply hold on to these simple-to-follow steps and helpful online flirting tips, and with proper timing, you are off to be a top online flirter. So you've been talking online, you're comfortable with someone and think you're ready to meet face-to-face. This is the exciting part, but how should you meet?

Meeting in Person

If you've been talking with a person and have gotten to feel comfortable with them, you might want to rush right out to meet them in person, but there are a few things you should keep in mind before you do. Remember, the only way you've gotten to know this person is through what they have told you. The only image you have is what photo they've posted or through a webcam. We're not saying they're being untruthful with you, but you need to keep yourself safe when meeting someone for the first time.

The most important thing is to meet in a public place preferably during the daylight hours. You don't want to meet a perfect stranger in a night when there's no one else around but you. Do not have them pick you up at home. Arrange for your transportation to the agreed-upon place. Make sure you have a full tank of gas in the event you need to make a getaway.

Arrive a little earlier than the pre-arranged time so you can take stock of the environment. Take note of where the doors are in case you have to make a quick exit. Also, find the nearest pay phone. They're often by the restrooms. Perhaps you can meet for coffee in a local café. Try a museum or art gallery for your first date. Go where there are going to be a lot of people. Bad things are less likely to happen if there's a crowd around you.

Why not consider a group date? Double dating can ease the anxiety you're going to feel and make you more at ease. Plus, you won't be alone with anyone and there will be many more chances for diverse conversation.

Don't plan to meet up without telling someone where you're going. Make sure a family member or friend knows what time your meeting is and where it will be. That way if anything should happen, they'll know where to find you.

Have an exit strategy. If the person makes you feel uneasy or you just plain don't like them, don't feel bad about leaving. After all, your safety comes first. If it feels wrong, get out! Carry a cell phone with you or have plenty of change for a pay phone. Not only can a cell phone be a lifesaver when it comes to getting away from a bad date, but you'll also want to be able to communicate with someone if something should go bad.

Never, ever, under any circumstances have them come to your home for your first meeting. While you might have a certain comfort level being in a familiar place, if this turns out to be not what you expected, you won't have a way to exit and no way to get them to leave aside from force, and we're pretty sure you don't want that to happen. Along the same line, don't meet at their home either. Stick to public places. It's better to be safe than sorry! Don't meet with someone until you are completely sure you want to. Some people may apply pressure to get together in person, but you have control and shouldn't do so until you are truly ready.

Once you are on the date, steer the conversation away from overly personal details. Just as if you were chatting online, you're meeting this person for the first time so try not to reveal specific things about your life. Keep it general – at least for now.

Pay close attention to any displays of violence or sudden outbursts. This could signal emotional problems that you certainly won't want to deal with. Also, be aware of any attempts to control or pressure you. As we said before, you should be comfortable and do only what feels right for you.

If possible, avoid drinking alcohol while on a date. Alcohol could affect your judgment and lessen your inhibitions. If you are drinking, keep the drink in your sight all the time. Do not get too drunk. You might not know what might happen later or remember what you have been doing.

Finally, just be alert and trust your instincts. Try to relax and enjoy this first meeting, but don't let your guard down too much. Safety is your first concern – for both you and your date.

Now that we've addressed the safety issues, you will want to make a good first impression.

CHAPTER TWELVE

A Successful First Date

The rules of dating have not changed much over the years. The purpose of a first date is and always has been a way of determining whether or not a second date is likely. A first date is not a make-or-break type of deal. If the pairing does not work out, the only thing that has been lost is time. If the time spent on the first date was even a bit enjoyable, then nothing was lost.

You may have been out of commission for a while and it's scary to think of going back into the dating pool. Seniors aren't the only ones who feel this way, so just relax and be yourself.

A first date is one of the most nerve-wracking aspects of dating at any age. If you're 50+ and just starting to date again after a few years or a few decades, however, the uncertainty about where to go, what to wear, and what to talk about can seem almost insurmountable.

You wonder whether your date will like you, whether you'll like him or her, and how much dating etiquette has changed since the last time you were out there.

When organizing that first date, try to think of activities that you would both enjoy doing together. You could plan a romantic picnic for two, visit a local art gallery, attend a play or concert or play golf or hike if you both like physical activities. A visit to a local winery makes a lovely afternoon as do book browsing and coffee if you both enjoy reading.

Maybe an afternoon matinee at the movies would fit you both, but couple it with an early or late lunch depending on the movie time. You want your first date activities to encourage conversation because, after all, the purpose is to see if you want a second date.

Check with your local senior centre and see if they have any activities planned that you and your date would enjoy. Many have organized day trips or dances specifically for senior singles. Don't make the date too complicated or jam-packed with activities. Make it easy and enjoyable for both of you!

Be sure to have a backup plan in case the original one doesn't work out. If you've planned to meet at a local outdoor music festival, but the rain postpones it, agree to meet at the nearby restaurant instead.

You should initially plan for a shorter date. One to two hours is sufficient. If things are going well, you can always extend the date, but there's no need to try and map out your whole lives together on the first date. You don't want to be stuck in an all-day event if you realize five minutes into the date that this person is wrong for you.

Be specific on a dress code for where you will be going. A cocktail dress for a fast food joint would just be awkward. A T-shirt and jeans for a four-star restaurant would just be inappropriate. It can be embarrassing when one person shows up in dress clothes and the other in casual.

Compliment your date, but don't overdo it. Everyone has something appealing about them – find that one thing and comment about it. A few nice words can make a person feel special, but persistent comments about looks, body, etc. can just be annoying.

Balance your talking with listening. The purpose of this meeting is to get to know each other a little better. You don't want to dominate the conversation with talk about yourself. Learn to listen and offer up details about your own life – just not too many!

Don't compare your date with your prior partner. Everyone has endearing qualities and no one will be quite like the one you are now without. Look for those good qualities in the person you're with.

The senior years don't give you the right to be boring. You have a lot to offer and a lot to share. Be sincere, and honest, and regain that charm you had when you dated as a young person.

And remember, it's OK these days to kiss on the first date. Avoid sex, however. While young people might think that's alright, sex on the first date remains tacky and inappropriate.

Men, try ending the date first and do it politely, though make sure that you show you're interested. This will make you stand out.

You may want to send an e-mail or instant message directly after the date ends just to say "thanks". Something short and sweet is fine – "I had a great time – thanks so much!" will suffice. However, if the date wasn't what you wanted, just stay away from the contact. No need to string the other person along down a dead-end road.

Women, don't wear anything provocative or too sexy. This sounds like an old cliché but first impressions last. Your date won't know anything about you except for how you look and how you behave. He will take you at face value and giving him the wrong impression of what sort of person you are is not something you want to do.

Try and wear clothing that makes you confident and that you are comfortable wearing. It will be uncomfortable enough without worrying about that tightness around your waist or the itchy necktie.

Ask your date about themselves. A healthy interest in getting to know your date is a good sign to show him/her. This means that you want to learn about him/her and think of your date as an interesting person.

Remember, the most interesting conversationalists are those who ask about others. Great topics are work, hobbies and sports. Just keep it light and conversational.

Try not to overdo the perfume or the cologne. If it's too strong, the scent can be quite distracting. It's very hard to complete an evening out with your date dazed by the smell.

Mouthwash is important. Also, brush your teeth and bring a couple of mints if you're eating out. Always remember... have fun and be yourself!

Though it may seem a bit intimidating to return to the social scene after many years, it can be a fun and rewarding experience for those in search of companionship. Just remember to find something you enjoy and odds are you'll meet other dating senior singles that share many of your interests and have a great first date!

What do you do if a date goes wrong?

Surviving a Bad Date

Occasionally, a bad date happens to everyone at a certain point in his or her life. You should do some assessment before writing off the person for life. Are there no sparks at all? Are they too nervous to open any topic? Is he or she being rude?

Here are some things that you can do to deal with a bad date or when you are the one who's about to make it bad.

If you are feeling too nervous opt for a date over coffee. You will have less time fidgeting due to over-nervousness since after finishing your coffee you can easily bid your date a quick adieu.

There is no excuse for a date that is obnoxious and rude. Walk away and let it be.

If you and your date are not on the same wavelength, it might not be working out. Endure the date, maintain your composure and leave politely. If your date asks for an extension like an after-meal drink, you can always politely say no.

If you unintentionally insult your date, simply apologize and move on. If your insult is not that severe, your date might just forgive and forget. The same goes if they unintentionally insult you. Realize that they are probably just as nervous as you are. You'll have to be the bigger one and forgive and forget.

Never provide entertainment at your expense. Humour is cool, self-bashing is not. It is not worth it to make yourself feel uncomfortable trying to impress your date. Avoid negativity and focus on your positive traits. If your date is going badly, what's a good way to exit gracefully? There are many – most of which involve little white lies, unfortunately.

If you are brave enough to tell it like it is, by all means do so. Honesty can be the best policy; however, it can also hurt the other person's feelings. If you want to avoid this, as most people do, you may be faced with making up a harmless story to spare your date's feelings. This story is up to you but make it plausible. Perhaps you suddenly don't feel well. Maybe you "forgot" to turn off your coffee pot.

You can also set up a pre-arranged time for a friend or family member to call you. If the date is going well, that's fine, but if it's not, this is the perfect out. You can have an "emergency" that just can't wait and explain it away by the phone call alerting you of such.

What do you do with those feelings that might arise from a date that has gone bad? Don't punish yourself for a date that went bad. Save it somewhere in your mind that is remote. Or better yet, commend yourself for being able to go through it. Learn from your mistakes. Share the details with a friend. This way, you can treat it more as a laughingstock than something that will haunt you for life.

Get occupied with other activities so you can forgive yourself and forget about the bad date. Exercising, eating something sweet or watching a movie will make the bad vibes go away sooner than you expect.

Honesty and kindness are a good combination when it comes to turning down a bad date that would like a second round. Say something a bit blunt but peppered with some praise. "You seem like a wonderful person, but you're just not for me."

Now, if you think that the person still deserves a second chance, by all means, give it a second try. You can always laugh the bad date incident away when you are more comfortable with each other.

Most of all, however, shake it off and get back online! There's bound to be someone else you can connect with. Dating isn't always an exact science. It might take a few tries to find that perfect one!

What if you find yourself in a situation where someone wants to go out with you but you don't want to go out with them?

Thanks, But No Thanks

It's easy to get caught up in a chat and become overly interested in being nice. If you've simply been being polite while chatting with someone, but they're interested in more, you're faced with a difficult task. Is there an easy way to say "I'm just not interested?" Not really.

The best advice we can give you is to just be honest. It's much better to be honest early on than to go out with someone just because you're "guilted" into it or just want to be nice. We're relatively sure that you wouldn't want someone to go out with you just to be nice. Why waste the time?

When turning someone down for a date, focus on what you don't have in common. Explain to them that you just don't like hanging out in smoky bars as they do and it just wouldn't be a fun time in your eyes.

The same applies if you don't get a phone call or e-mail for a second date. Often, men think they're supposed to wait a while before calling a woman for a second date. This is rude, but for women, you need to realize that maybe he's just not that into you.

Calling him up and expressing your rage at his rudeness is just plain wrong. It can cause you to have a bad reputation and result in added stress that you just don't need. There are hundreds of others online that you try to connect with. Get back out there and shake it off.

Alternatively, men, you should be aware that just because a woman shows a little interest, she might be faking it. Many women find it difficult to turn a man down for a date or a second date, but if she's honest with you, accept it and move on. Perhaps – on the flip side – she's just not that into you!

Don't string someone along just because you're too polite to say no. It's better, to be honest, and move along rather than waste any more time with someone you know you won't be compatible with.

One thing that seniors have difficulty with when entering the dating world is the reactions of their friends and family. How does the dating senior address this?

I've Met Someone

Family members – especially children – can be overly critical when it comes to a new relationship for you. They have their issues with the loss of their prior partner whether it is through death or divorce, so it's especially problematic when you've found someone you want to pursue a relationship with.

The reaction of grown children to their parent dating again can be one of the biggest obstacles you face. It's hard enough for them to picture their mom and dad in a romantic liaison in their heyday – it's especially difficult for them to see you as a vibrant, healthy, sexual being.

Some grown children simply have a difficult time understanding that their parents are real human beings with the same feelings and needs as younger singles, so they may tend to discourage any budding romance.

These same grown children may also be reacting out of concern for their parents, feeling a need to protect him/her from being taken advantage of. This may certainly be a valid concern, but if the senior in question is of a sound and healthy mind, interference should be minimal at best.

You need to concentrate on yourself and what's best for you. Hopefully, you have a good enough relationship with your children to be able to talk openly and honestly about your desire to continue living instead of waiting to die.

Explain to them that having a person in your life other than them is important to you. Tell them that you still have a lot of living to do and you don't want to do it alone.

Often your grown children may feel like a potential date is using you or simply after your financial assets. Reassure them that you will be very careful in this area and you will not be taken advantage of.

Ultimately, you have to think about yourself and what will make you happy. Sure, the opinion of your children is important to you, but your opinion of yourself needs to be at the forefront.

Your children are grown and they have lives of their own. Point out to them that you have worked hard to get where you are and dating is important for you to feel needed, wanted, and alive.

Display your confidence in yourself and your dating abilities. Show them that you know what you are doing and that, despite their misgivings, you will be just fine. You've earned the right to be happy and you are going for it!

Believe it or not, attracting the person you want is a state of mind. Let's look at how you can attract that right person – in general.

CHAPTER THIRTEEN

The Rules of Attraction

Do you wish you could attract exactly who you want? Do you want to have more dates and more choices? Would you like to meet the person of your dreams? Perhaps you need to discover the rules of attraction.

There are essentially five rules that will bring you more of what you want: more choices, more love, and more happiness. If you are looking for a relationship, concentrate on these rules of attraction. Following these rules puts you in control of your destiny.

First, look for signs of love. Change your negative picture that love does not exist. Since your thoughts become your reality, you need to look for signs of love between a man and a woman.

If you do not think love happens except in the movies, it may take you a while to see it in others. But it is out there. You can start writing down the positive examples of love that you see. This will become your book of evidence that you can refer to when you get discouraged. These new examples become some of your new thoughts.

Believe that you will find love. If you believe that you can find your mate, you will. If you believe that you can't, you won't. Other people have found their soul mate...you can too.

Focus on what it is that you want. We get what we focus on. Think about what kind of relationship you would like to have. Dream big.

Make a list of the top ten qualities you would like to have in another. Whenever your thoughts and feelings go to hopeless, change your thoughts. Cut pictures out of a magazine that shows a man and a woman enjoying their time together, whether walking on a beach or sharing a candlelit dinner. Post these pictures in a place where you can see them often. When you look at them several times a day, see yourself in that picture.

Surround yourself with a vision of the relationship you want. When you look at pictures of couples having fun, or when you see others enjoying each other, imagine that you are doing the same. Feel it happening to you. See yourself having the relationship you have always wanted.

Probably the most important rule of attraction is to become the kind of person you want to find. You attract who you are. What kind of person do you want to find? Are you that person? Get busy becoming the wonderful person you would like to share your life with. If you are depressed or despairing, get help.

Remember to fill yourself with positive energy by doing activities that you love. Sort out your finances, handle your past baggage, make your living environment something you are proud of that gives you peace and comfort, and surround yourself with friends and family members who support you. It is from this space that you create someone who will love you.

And finally, be generous – to yourself and others. We find someone to love when we love ourselves in a kind and nurturing way. You deserve to love and be loved. And remember, someone awaits you.

Now that we've addressed the basic issues and concerns in online dating, let's look at some general dating tips for seniors – both men and women!

Attracting Women

Dating is not easy for everyone. To some, it could be an exciting and fun activity that allows them to meet other people, and maybe even their potential life partner! But for others, this ritual can feel like a slow and painful torture, leading to an execution; especially for those men who do not have much luck when it comes to attracting women.

But there are ways you can attract women and realize that they might be interested. It doesn't have to be as difficult as you think it might be.

When in person, read body language. Chances are, she's putting out signals that she's interested. Some tell-tale signs of interest include:

- Biting her lips
- Twirling her hair
- Gazing at you
- Touching her face
- Laughing and touching you

Whether online or in person, be approachable and open to conversation. Be friendly and ask questions. Smile a lot when in person. Convey that smile when online. You can do this through positive comments and talking about yourself and the person you are chatting with.

When face-to-face, it's important to be clean and presentable. Women are not going to go for guys who have poor grooming habits. When going out, men should always wear clean clothes, comb their hair, and never douse themselves after shaving. A little is okay, but a lot can be too much to take, and may send the women scurrying away in the other direction!

When you're over 50, you may notice the presence of an abnormal amount of ear or nose hair. Keep these areas trimmed and clean. It's a real turn-off to see these errant hairs sticking out when trying to keep up an interesting conversation.

Make eye contact, too. There's nothing more attractive and sexy than having someone look directly into their eyes while they are talking with them. They say the eyes are the window to the soul. There's no better way to connect with a woman than to give her a glimpse into your soul.

Finally, have something clever to say. Women love men with great personalities and this can be conveyed through what you say. If the woman you're talking with has a love of literature, quote something from a well-known book. If she loves the theatre, refer to the amazing symbolism in her favourite play. You'll not only win her heart but her respect as well.

And no matter what people may tell you – chivalry is not dead and women DO appreciate it. This is especially true for seniors. Senior women remember the day when a man opened the door for a woman and let her enter a room first. Pull her chair out for her at a restaurant and help her put on her coat. While feminism is still alive and well, all women love to be pampered and remembering these tried and true techniques will impress her – trust me!

What about you women?

Attracting Men

So many women – especially senior women – are in search of Mr Right. Women tend to live longer than men, so some women think that the pickings might be slim when they reach a certain age. This is far from the truth. There are ways to find and attract that special guy. But some obstacles stand in your way.

First and foremost, you need to get rid of that extra baggage you're carrying around with you. Past relationships can affect future relationships, but don't let them. What happened in the past is the past. You don't have to dwell on it and let it be part of your present or your future.

Many women have low self-esteem which can influence the attractive qualities that are naturally inside them. You need to change your way of thinking here and convince yourself that you're worthy of a good relationship to complement everything that you are.

Low self-esteem is an aspect of your personality that has been cultivated over years and years. Let go and let yourself be that wonderful person that lives inside of you.

Tell yourself positive things including that you deserve to be loved and you deserve to continue living a healthy and full life. Confidence is the ultimate sexy trait in women, but avoid being too confident. A little humility is sexy as well.

If you think there just aren't any good men out there, you're wrong. This is a belief that has been bantered around for years. Some of this is rooted in past experiences. Still more is because you've set your expectations too high. No one is perfect and if you expect to find someone who is perfect, you'll be disappointed. As a mature woman, you have many great qualities that you should embrace and use to your advantage.

Remember when you were in the first throes of a new romance, and all of a sudden you got hit on a lot? That's because you radiated self-confidence; you were loved. Now, in your mature adult years, you should have plenty of self-confidence in your ability to balance a job, the ex, the children, the bank account, the ageing parents, friends, etc.

Self-confidence is the biggest turn-on and once you've reached 50, you've got plenty of it.

You've been there and done that too! Now you know what you like. You are a better lover than you were at 20 because you know what turns you on, and you should be comfortable telling your partner exactly what you need.

Indulge yourself. And if you feel like you have to be demure and shy, get rid of that! You have the right to be a strong, sensual woman – even as a senior citizen. You don't have to be that coy little chanteuse anymore. Assert yourself and enjoy the results!

Older women tend to be more daring as well. They're the ones signing up for all that adventure travel. Odds are you'll find more older women than men on cruises to the Antarctic, treks through Nepal and gorilla-watching expeditions in Africa.

Women are more liberated when the kids move out and allow them to reclaim the lives they put on hold decades ago with their first delivery. This liberation is empowering and can be very alluring.

Read the section above on how men can attract women and employ these strategies. If you're interested in a man, look him in the eye, touch him lightly on the hand, twirl your hair (if possible) and make him know that you want to know more about him!

Above all, exude comfort with yourself. Know that you deserve to find love and companionship and let him know that. When you are confident, you will be stronger and that's what surviving in the dating world is all about.

We're getting ready to tread on controversial territory next, but we feel like we need to address the obvious outcome that is likely to come from dating and relationships. Can seniors have a vibrant and satisfying sex life? Absolutely!

CHAPTER FOURTEEN

Seniors and Sex

Many older adults and seniors report that their sex lives improve as they age. Once the children are grown and work doesn't require the energy it used to, couples can relax together and enjoy each other without the old distractions. They find that the senior sex gets better.

When we're talking about sex and online dating, we do feel compelled to tell you that you should never, ever do anything sexually that you aren't comfortable with. Do not, under any circumstances, feel that you must have sex with someone just because they took you out on a date. However, if you feel the urge, and the time is right, there are some steps you can take to insure the sex is awesome – even at your age!

Communication is the key to real intimacy. As your body changes in your senior years, it's important to communicate your thoughts, feelings, fears, and desires with your partner. Encourage your partner to communicate fully with you, too. Improving your communication will help both of you feel closer and can make senior sex more pleasurable.

If you would like to try something new, discuss it with your partner, and be open to his or her ideas. The senior years, when you have more time and fewer distractions, can be a time of creativity and passion. Sometimes just talking about sex can make you feel sexy.

Think about sex in a new way. As a senior, you might not be as comfortable with some sexual positions as you once were, but this does not mean you need to give up an activity that is pleasurable for you and miss out on feeling close to your partner.

Senior sex calls for creativity. Try different positions to find ones that please you and your partner. If erectile dysfunction is an issue, try intercourse with the woman on top, where hardness is less important. Experiment with positions that you both find comfortable and pleasurable. Make your senior years a time of sexual generosity and sharing.

Expand your sexual play beyond intercourse. Holding each other, gentle touching, kissing, and sensual massage are all ways to share passionate feelings. You might experiment with oral sex and masturbation as ways to please each other in bed.

Keep your mind and body healthy. If you exercise regularly and eat a healthy, balanced diet, you'll look and feel better for yourself – and your partner. And a healthy body will help you enjoy senior sex, no matter what your age. Keep fruits and vegetables high on your list, and limit the amount of alcohol you consume. Too much alcohol can decrease sexual function in both men and women.

Check with your healthcare provider to design a workout plan for yourself, and stick to it. Stretching, aerobics for your heart and strength training will all help you feel sexier and improve your stamina and flexibility."And don't underestimate the appeal of an active mind. Find activities you enjoy that stimulate your intellect and imagination, and share them with your partner. Seniors who enjoy their lives have their special sexiness.

For all adults, not just seniors, medications and illness can affect your sexual drive. If you have questions about how prescriptions will affect senior sexuality, check with your healthcare provider. If you notice any sexual problems, seek medical help as soon as possible. Your healthcare provider may be able to help you stay fit and active, as long as you're willing to talk about what's bothering you.

Finally, be true to yourself. Try to let go of expectations and things you think you should do as you enter your senior years. If you enjoyed an active sex life when you were younger, there's no reason to slow down with age, unless you want to. On the other hand, if you are not especially turned on by sex but want to feel close to your partner, communicate your desires and find activities that please both of you.

Is there a time of day when you have the most energy? That's the optimal time for sex. Mornings are often good if you're refreshed from sleep but anytime is fine if it works for you and your partner. If you find in your senior years that it takes longer to become sexually aroused, start lovemaking with a romantic dinner – or breakfast. Share romantic or erotic literature and poetry, hold hands, touch often, and don't be shy about saying what you love about each other.

You may have intercourse less often than you used to, but the closeness and love will still be there. Be creative, loving, open-minded, and willing to communicate with your partner. You'll find it's possible to enjoy senior sex at any age. Well, that's about it for the tips and tricks. We do, however, want to let you know about some common online abbreviations you might encounter during your conversations.

Concluding Thoughts

Just because you've crossed over into the senior set doesn't mean you can't have a healthy and satisfying dating life. Growing older doesn't mean growing slower. Nobody grows old merely by living many years. We grow old by deserting our ideals. Years may wrinkle the skin, but to give up enthusiasm wrinkles the soul.

You are in the prime of your life – even if society doesn't think so. Well, show them! Embrace the fact that you are ready to re-enter the world of romance and love by finding that other special someone.

In these past few years, the trend in dating from all over the world has changed drastically. Individuals looking to meet people don't choose to line up in queues anymore, to try to get into the hottest places. Seldom will they be seen hanging out in pubs and bars, trying to catch a glimpse of prospective hook-ups.

Online dating is the perfect venue to do this in. You don't have the awkwardness of struggling through meeting someone and then trying to charm them. You can charm them with your words and typing without worrying about how you look or how you act. Now singles can meet and greet each other without leaving the refuge of their homes. Sounds crazy, but now this is the most preferred way individuals socialize.

Online dating is fun -- if you know how to play. Some rules abound and courtesy should be exercised so you won't offend the other party. Try to be sincere, but not to a point that you appear vulnerable and come off as an easy scam target. Most of all, have fun. It's a dating site, for crying out loud!

You can get to know someone first and then take it from there.

Conclusion

Many of my readers might be worried that everything does not work out like has been described, what would they do? Or in other words, if this first date does not work out, what should they do? The answer is very simple, repeat the whole process!

Let's go back to where we started. Remember, this is a chance to find a partner for life so we might have to grow many plants before we get the right harvest. I am not talking about two-timing here. What I mean is that instead of putting all your eggs in one basket, keep the avenues open. Don't just bank on one person, because if that doesn't work out, you might lose heart. You can hope for the best but expect the contrary as well.

Only the very lucky ones get the right pick on the first go. For the rest of us, we just have to keep trying till we succeed. Another advantage of trying out different people is that you can get to choose. It should not be that you just flipped for the first guy or girl who came your way. Take your time, give yourself some breathing space and then make the right decision.

Nobody can force you into making a commitment. It should be completely your choice. Of course, if you get the right cues and something deep down inside tells you that this is the right person for you, then what are you waiting for, go ahead and show the green signal.

But on the other hand, if someone is trying to force you into making a commitment and you feel hard-pressed, gently try to break away. All you have to do is put your foot down very firmly and tell the person that you need more time. However, it is not good to keep a person waiting indefinitely. Tell the person that you need perhaps a week or more than that. But don't let the person realize that you are checking out other people. Just tell them that this is probably the most important decision in your life so you just want to be sure.

I would like to add one word about signing off. In case things do not work out please take care to part gracefully. In such instances, it is not the best decision to say such things over chat. The other person may put forward some very uncomfortable questions that you will have a tough time answering.

The best thing you could do is send the person an e-mail telling him or her that he or she was not really what you had in mind, but you would like to remain, good friends, all the same.

You do not have to worry about being pestered by the other person in future; the "good friends" part never fails. Most people dislike being called a good friend after a close encounter. In most cases, the relationship just fizzles out after this. However please remember that it is indeed bad manners to part without a word and just stop answering emails without any information at all. Some people do that because they do not want to offend the other person. But such callousness is really bad.

So that is all about it. You know everything that is to be known and the ball is now well and truly in your courts. So what are you waiting for, why don't you go out there and make your presence felt and come back with the catch of a lifetime? I don't think that we have left any stones unturned and from here I'm sure that on your first date, everything will be well in your control.

…y Libri Plureos GmbH in Hamburg,
Germany